Proof - Read Copy.
Sell for charity only.
Chris Firth 2024

GW00391782

The Folklore of British Insects

2nd edition

The Folklore of British Insects

Astonishing facts, myths, and legends of the creepy-crawlies of Great Britain

Words: Chris Firth
Illustrations: Rebecca Hobbs

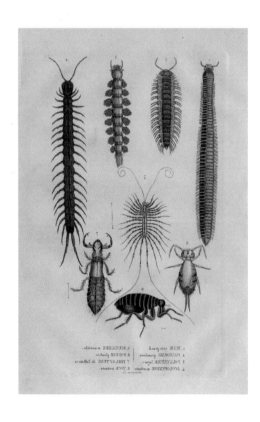

Folklore, urban myths, classical mythology, medicinal cures, practical uses, scary facts and cooking tips – you will never look at your fleas and bedbugs in the same light again!

Electraglade Press © 2024

:
Insects and their relatives - Hexapoda

There are roughly five million living species of insects on this planet, with a huge variety of behaviours and body forms. It is estimated that there is a quintillion of individual insects alive in the world at any one moment. That's:
1 000 000 000 000 000 000
for those who prefer numbers to words. There may be a couple of million more or less either way here and there.

Apart from being astoundingly beautiful, amazing in their variety of forms and structures, and endlessly fascinating, insects are essential to the planet, and to humans. They pollinate crops, break down waste debris in the soil, eliminate pest species and are food for many other animals (including, as you will see, humans). Every ecosystem in the natural world depends upon insects. As well as these natural benefits they provide humans with products such a honey, wax, silk, dyes, protein and medicines.

The Hexapoda classification translates from the Greek as 'six footed', so technically there are creatures in this book that are not insects as such, but we have included them for their creepy-crawliness. If you come to, or do already, love insects as much as we do here, you will agree that they are not 'creepy' at all in the negative sense. However, there is no point in not using a brilliant phrase of metaphoric alliteration in a subtitle just because of personal tastes and perceptions. And after all, they literally do creep and crawl, and fly, and bore and drill and penetrate every minute and dank, dark corner of the natural world.

A Disclaimer

Of course, countless insects and creepy crawlies have not made it into this book, and we apologise for that. We are limited by space and time, whereas the insect world is not. So, apologies if we have missed out your particular favourite bug. We completely disassociate ourselves, legally, from any of the recipes or folk cures that you might choose to try which are detailed in this book. So, if you do poison yourselves on snails, dragonflies or cockroaches, or any other insect mentioned, or sting yourself to death trying out bee-acupuncture, please do not attempt to sue us. This book is intended to be informational, not instructional.

We hope you enjoy buzzing, picking and skittering around the pages that await you here.

Ants
Bedbugs
Bees
Beetles
Butterflies and Caterpillars
Centipedes
Cockroaches
Dragonflies
Earwigs
Fleas
Flies
Glow worms
Grasshoppers and Crickets
Ladybirds
Scorpions
Slugs and Snails
Silverfish
Spiders
Wasps
Woodlice
Worms

Ants - Formicidae

Eurymedusa, seduced by the god Zeus who appeared to her as an ant, bore him a son, who was named Aeacus. Aeacus was born on an island far to the north of Greece, which even back then was known as Britannia. In those days the island was uninhabited, and once Aeacus's mother had left him to fend for himself there were no servants to cook or clean or tidy for him. He wailed and he moaned and he wept and he groaned. Eventually, his father, the mighty Zeus, took pity on him. Seeing that there were no men or even animals yet on the islands thereabouts, but that many insects lived and thrived, Zeus wove some magic. All the ants on the islands were transformed into men and women. A whole new race, the Myrmidons, was formed, and their whole duty and purpose was to serve and look after poor Aeacus. He became their ruler and vowed that he would look after his new tribe despite his lack of knowledge about the world of men and the ways and workings of the gods. And so, at last, the islands of Britain were inhabited by humans, and for better or for worse, the descendants of Zeus, Eurymedusa and Aeacus still inhabit the islands of Great Britain to this very day.

Some Ant Folklore

Ants are symbolic of hard work, perseverance, diligence and community spirit.
If you dream of black ants, good health and unexpected wealth are sure to follow.
If you dream of red ants expect bad luck. Unless you dream of them leaving your house in a long stream bearing their Queen's eggs – this is a good sign.
'Don't tread on an ant – it's done nothing to you!' – Adam Ant
If you discover an ant nest in your home and do not want it there, simply ask them to leave. Ask them politely but firmly. Within two days they will have gone. Apparently, this is guaranteed.

Of Ants and Bulls

Daedalus, father of Icarus, was given the task of threading a fine golden wire through a spiraling seashell. If he failed in the task, the King of Minos, who suspected Daedalus of being a murderer, would have him and his son put to most gruesome deaths. Daedalus, being somewhat clever, found an ant and tied the golden thread around its tiny waist. He then put a blob of honey on the tip of the conical shell and placed the ant inside. Attracted by the scent of the honey, the ant crawled and scrambled its way around the coils of the shell. Sure enough, it eventually popped out from the tip of the shell and began to feast on the honey. Daedalus picked it up and drew the thread through the shell, releasing the ant with its reward of honey as he did so. King Minos was baffled and astounded that Daedalus had been able to complete the task. He spared him and his son and employed him to design and build a great labyrinth, in which he would imprison the half-bull, half-human monster child of his unfaithful wife – The Minotaur.

Ants as Food

Can you eat ants? Of course you can. You can even buy tinned ants in Thailand – order online now! As larvae and adults, they are used as human food in many parts of the world. Ants are high in protein value, high in levels of antioxidants so helpful for bowel problems, are plentiful, and are easy to find in cities or in the wild. The Asian weaver ant is particularly favoured as a delicacy in Thailand and Laos. The 'big bottomed ant' of Columbia is a delicacy as highly prized and valued as caviar in Europe. Well, if you would eat raw fish eggs why not eat lightly seasoned ants? The pregnant queen ants, bloated with eggs hence their colloquial name of 'big-butts', are roasted and said to taste like peanuts, popcorn or crispy bacon. Packets of them can be bought on street corners and they feature on the menus of high-end restaurants throughout Columbia. A similar delicacy is popular in some parts of Cornwall, where the milder climate leads to bigger ants. 'Queen Ant Muffin' is said to be popular in Penzance.

Bees – Apoidea

'A swarm of bees in May
Is worth a load of hay
But a swarm of bees in July
Is hardly worth a fly.'

There are already countless books about bees (a hive of books!). The magical, beneficial properties of bees and the restorative and healing power of honey is known world-wide, and the space here can barely do the topic justice. There are myths in almost every culture of the world associating bees with the sacred and divine - in eastern and Aegean cultures the bee was believed to be the insect that links the natural world to the underworld, and priestesses in many ancient cultures were referred to as 'bees.' In Greek mythology, Apollo's gift of prophecy came from three bee goddesses, identified with the Thriae, who had the head and upper body of a beautiful woman and the lower body of a bee. Apart from bestowing powers upon Apollo, they liked to drink honey and dust their hair with pollen.

Some Bee Folklore

Bees have long been regarded as messengers of the gods. Hive and beekeepers (apiarists) whispered family news and local gossip to the hives. If they neglected to this the bees would become disgruntled and fly away, taking the valuable future commodity of honey with them. Apiarists are well aware that bees respond to different tones of the human voice, and they will not stay long with a grumpy, snappy, harsh-toned beekeeper. It has long been the custom to inform the hives of a death in the family, and again, it was believed that if this was not done, the bees would fly away. A family member, such as the widow, or heir, would knock three times on each hive with an iron key and tell the bees of the departed soul. Black crepe or ribbons would be tied around the hives to remind the bees that someone close had departed from this life and to inform passers-by that the bees were in mourning.

The British Celts were one of the many races for whom bees were held sacred. They believed them to be possessed of great wisdom, and similarly to eastern cultures, thought that they travelled to the Otherworld to bring back messages from the gods. It is said that the Celts originally only came north to the British islands in search of 'the black bee' and its valuable, happiness inducing honey. Back then bees swarmed and flew in vast numbers everywhere in Britain, and the Welsh bards referred to the land as The Isles of Honey. In the Western Isles of Scotland bees were long associated with the wisdom and ways of the Druids, and people believed that bees had secret knowledge and powers. There is a saying there – 'ask the wild bee of what the druid knew.' Highlanders believed that while in deep sleep or in a music induced trance, a person's soul would temporarily leave the body in the form of a bee and visit the Otherworld.

Inevitably, bees became acquisitioned by the Christian faith. There are folk beliefs in Scotland and northern England that bees in every hive would hum loudly at midnight on Christmas day, singing a hymn to celebrate the birth of Jesus. Bees in Cornwall could only ever be moved in their hives on Good Friday, and it a fact that even today beehives can only ever be moved three feet or three miles, in respect of the Holy Trinity. It is no coincidence that the solitary retreats (clochans), of the Irish hermit monks were shaped like beehives and known as beehive huts. And let's not forget Samson's, pre-haircut, puzzling honey from the beehive in a lion that he had killed by hand, illustrated on every British treacle tin:

'Out of the eater came forth meat, and out of the strong came forth sweetness.' Judges 14:14

Bees, Honey and Medicine

There are too numerous cures, benefits, magical and medicinal properties of honey to go into here. In short, honey or honey-based products such as mead and the renowned, body-transforming royal jelly, can cure just about anything. There is even a technical, scientific word for bee cures and the art of healing with bees – Apitherapy.

Bee stings, applied like ancient Chinese acupuncture to specific points on the body, are said to be a beneficial cure for rheumatism and arthritis. Applied in the correct way, bee stings and venom boost the immune system and are said to be good for healing anything from migraines to male erectile dysfunction. A word of caution, however, before thinking of stinging yourself or others with bees for medicinal purposes. People are reported to have died during 'live bee acupuncture' after suffering anaphylactic shock reactions, having not realised before trying out the treatment that they had an acute allergy to bee stings.

Bees as Food

In Indonesia bees eaten within the honeycomb are considered a delicacy. These are juvenile, stingless baby bees though. To eat adult bees could be hazardous as they contain venom and can sting the throat, which is likely to cause an aphylactic shock reaction in some people, a stung and swollen throat in others. It is perhaps best not to eat them though as bees pollinate over two thirds of the world's crop species and contribute to over one third of the food products that humans consume. Without them – and they are under threat through insecticides – crops would disappear and many in the world would starve. Sticking to eating or drinking just honey products is the best option for the planet with regard to 'bee food' - so on that note here is a traditional British dish to help you along the way.:

Lancashire Buzzing Oat Biscuits

Ingredients: 75g self-raising flour, 75g porridge oats, 75g caster or light brown sugar, 75g butter,

1 generous tablespoon of honey, a splash of full milk or cream. A small pinch of cinnamon, nutmeg or hinger. A level teaspoon of black treacle (optional).

Method: **Preheat the oven to 180 C/Gas 4 and place parchment on a baking tray.**

1. Sift the flour into a bowl - add the oats and sugar – mix.

2. Melt the butter, milk and honey together in an iron saucepan until it is a liquid. Add flour mixture and stir well together.

3. Form into biscuit shapes (around 12) and place in oven for around 12 to 15 minutes.

   Warning! The baking smell is tantalizing, and the biscuits taste delicious, so best double the ingredient amounts above if you have an appetite. Don't worry about eating too many though – they contain everything that is good and healthy.

hand to put in the stand and collect the delicious honey. Stupidly, the devil does so for as everybody now knows wasps do not produce honey. A giant wasp, The Wasp King, angrily appears from the nest and proceeds to sting the devil all over, driving him back to Hell. The farmer then attempts to persuade the obviously magical wasp. If he could convince him to grant a donkey that would spill silver coins from its mouth every time that it brayed. The Wasp King, somewhat irritated by the annoying and foolish farmer, stung the farmer to death and went to live in a crack in an elm tree. The soul, who started all the trouble anyway, moves away to Hamburg where he leads a life of pleasure as an unapologetic glutton. Oh - those Brothers Grim. No happy ending there then.

Late nineteenth and early twentieth century depictions of the Wasp King with a Santa hat on are of American origin, and these were largely to promote a brand of cola - McCarthy's Cola (Pennsylvania, around 1880 - The cola with a sting in its tail). The Christmas Wasp and the Wasp King are now largely forgotten about with McCarthy's Cola - the company (were bankrupt by 1921 soon after their Christmas Wasp advertising campaign.

Some Top Wasp Tips

The best way to treat a wasp sting is to dab it with baking powder or apply a paste of the same and avoid rubbing or scratching the affected area.

Unless you are handy, do not try to remove wasps' nest yourself. If unsuccessful you will be attacked by a swarm of wasps and chased by them as far as you can run. Get an expert in.

Bed Bugs - Cimex lectularius

'Bed Bug
Beddy Bug
Why be it me that you do hug?
Please don't bite me in the night,
I need to sleep all snug and tight.'

Traditional skipping rhyme, Yorkshire.

Some facts and folklore

Also known as the True Bed Bug. Like fleas and lice, these little bloodsuckers have always aroused fear and loathing in people. Although they are not so widespread in Great Britain now, many parts of the world and Europe are still infested with them. Like vampires, the True Bed-bugs are nocturnal. They hide behind pictures, in cracks in the floorboards and, of course, in beds. Beneath the sheets, under the pillows and inside teddy bears – that's where you'll find them! They feed on human blood but are equally happy to feed on pets and domestic animals. Their bite is quite painful although not always felt through the depths of sleep. It is usually in the morning after that the bites are noticed – painful, red, swollen spots at the bite-sites. Bed-bugs will continue to breed away in modern, warm centrally heated houses. If you want to get rid of them from a dwelling, you must open the windows, let in chilly air and keep the house at under 12 degrees centigrade for a couple of weeks. Brrrr! But no more bugs or bites.

How Bed Bugs Became

Once the laziest town in England was in the southwest of England – some say it was Bath, others say Bridport. Whichever, the folk there enjoyed the paradise of their locality. They liked to sleep in late and rarely got up before noon to tend their farms, shops, or gardens. The fields started to run riot and go to seed but still the folk slept in late – there was plenty of fruit on the trees and fish in the streams so there was no real need for farming and working.

The town mayor did not like to see the place looking scruffy and neglected. He decided to do something about it so went to see the old wise woman in the heart of the woods. She said she could help him – for a small fee – and off she slipped away into the trees. Some hours later she returned with a red velvet sack that seemed to be squirming and shimmering and writhing all about.

'Open this in the market square at mid-day on the next full moon and you'll see a change in the lazy rascals!' she said, laughing. He asked her what was in in the sack, but she just tapped her nose. 'I'll be knowing, but you'll soon see. Now give me my gold guinea and hop on your way.'

On the next full moon, at mid-day, at the cross in the market square, the mayor opened the red velvet sack, as instructed. The townsfolk were milling about, having just crawled out of their beds and thinking that they might get a bit of shopping in before their afternoon snooze. From the sack there leapt, swarmed and scurried a river of tiny red bed bugs with some black-flies and lice and other bitey-bed-creatures mixed in amongst them. Some hopped straight onto the clothing of the lazy townsfolk, others swarmed away into the cottages and farmsteads. Of course, these creatures, once at home in the beds and furnishings of the townsfolk, bit them and tickled them and harried them the whole nights through. Within a month the red-spotted folk were hopping out their beds at first light to be free of the biting. Soon the gardens were tended, the fields were mended, the shops were opened the town became the busiest, most active town in Britain – not so much because the folk there like to work, but they are fussy about whom they share their beds with.

'Night night, sleep tight
Mind the bed bugs don't bite.'

Beetles – Coleoptera

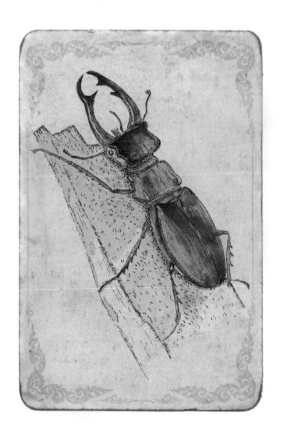

There are about 400 000 species of beetles, so we will not cover them all here in this little book. Beetles make up 40% of all insect species – there are a lot of them about! Beetles are important in folklore. The ancient Egyptian sacred scarab, dung-pushing beetle is well known of course; the scarab headed god was known as Kepri. According to some mythologies a beetle created the Milky Way. The Egyptians believed that a divine scarab beetle rolls the sun before it to cause it to rise and set, a simple creature powering our universe. They are great garden protectors and pollinators, almost as busy as bees.

In the Far East beetle wings were commonly used in art works of textiles, paintings, clothing and jewelry – the metallic iridescence of their wings is durable and long lasting and often long outlasts the paint and fabric dyes surrounding them. The colouration of beetles is created by transparent polymers, not pigments, - the colour is light refracting and refracting from physical, crystal-like structures in their 'skin', which means that their colours do not fade, even after death. This has been of huge interest to developers of car paints and cosmetics, who are now trying to embed this wonderful property of colouration into their paints and products.

A swarm of beetles in flight indicates that a storm is coming. Apparently, it is a sign of bad luck if a beetle walks over your shoe, and in medieval England this was considered as an omen of a death in the family. Of course, it is very unlucky for a beetle to walk under your shoe. This is definitely not good, and potentially is very unlucky for the beetle.

Some Beetle Folklore

A male stag beetle, Lucanus Cervus, that hefty pincered, dangerous looking lumberer, if worn on a hat, is said to give protection from lightning and 'the evil eye'. The reasoning was that this species is somehow connected to Thor, the god of thunder. If used correctly, with the right incantations, the owner of the hat could summon thunder and lightning to smite down his enemies. If kept in an inner jacket pocket, it was believed that a female stag beetle (with her much shorter mandibles) could attract wealth and good fortune, especially at the card or roulette table. In medieval times it was believed that stag beetles flew at night with hot coals in their jaws, setting fire to buildings, and especially churches, doing the work of the Devil. For this sinister reason they were banned from houses, castles and cottages and there was a fine for tenants if one was ever discovered under their rugs or floorboards. In British folklore a Devil's Coach-horse beetle, something of a disgusting wretch at the best of times, ate the core of Eve's dropped apple in the garden of Eden. Thus, endowed with eternal life, it still roams the planet to this day. It is believed that whoever finds this beetle and manages to crush it to death will be forgiven any or all of the seven deadly sins and guaranteed a place in Heaven. However, as tempting as a free ticket into Heaven might seem, the Devils Coach-horse is best well avoided and left alone. It usually dwells in excrement or dead bodies, emits a nasty nostril-stinging odour if disturbed and has a very painful bite. Even by pointing its tail at you it can draw on bad luck. There is a rumour that back in the 1970's, a colony of Devil's Coach-horses developed a taste for human flesh and went on the rampage in several villages in Suffolk, devouring numerous yokels before they were repelled by the army with blow-torches. This true story (according to Lorraine Fisher, 34, Literary Editor of The Suffolk Gazette) was turned into a novel by the writer, Richard Lewis.

Sex and The Blister Beetle

The Blister Beetle is poisonous, but commonly used as an aphrodisiac and cherished by men as a cure for erectile dysfunction down the ages – the first 'Viagra', in fact. Allegedly, women also find that it boosts their libido and sex drive. Crushed, soaked and diluted, it can be used to cure urinary infections, insect bites, kidney problems, burn and scalds of all kinds, and painful blisters. This beautiful emerald-green beetle is more commonly known as The Spanish Fly. There are many online testimonies to its uses and benefits, and it is said to have rescued many a faltering relationship from the doldrums.

Butterflies and Moths – Lepidoptera

Some Interesting Butterfly Facts

An ancient symbol of the soul, of rebirth, hope and the afterlife in cultures right around the world, most people love butterflies and delight in seeing them. Harbingers of the sun, summer, fertility and good luck, what child has not laughed at the fluttering sky-dance of a butterfly? Worldwide there are over 20 000 species of butterfly, although alas diminishing by the year. In the British Isles there are 57 resident species and two regular visitors – the Painted Lady and Clouded Yellow. Along with bees they are essential pollinators – if they continue to decline in these small islands as well as world-wide, the survival of some human food crops are at risk.

Most butterflies are very short lived, just a few weeks or so, in their final, mating *butterfly* phase. Of course, they have already had an existence as a hungry feeding caterpillar and a transformative metamorphic state as a cocooned chrysalis (or *pupa*). Butterflies taste out sugary nectars and nutritional liquids with their feet. Their wings are actually transparent, the colours we see caused by thousands of miniature, well positioned scales, like pretty sequins on a dress. The transparent scales reflect and refract light to create the colours we perceive in our visual spectrum, which are in fact for defensive, camouflaging purposes and possibly mating signals. Lepidoptera is Greek, meaning 'scaly wing'. Their beautiful colours and wing patterns are literally just a trick of the light.

Only in English is the fluttering colourful winged creature's name connected with 'butter', and there is no convincing explanation of why this is so. They were apparently called 'buterfleoge' in Old English, which has allegedly become corrupted into our modern version, 'butterfly'. There is some half-churned theory that in medieval folklore butterflies were thought to be witches who transformed themselves into tiny, winged creatures to steal milk and butter in country dairies, but this explanation seems very tenuous and a little cheesy so fortunately has not become widespread.

Some Butterfly Folklore and Superstitions

Butterflies are symbolically linked to the human soul. According to the Greeks, Psyche, Cupid's lover and the goddess of the soul, was made immortal in the form of a butterfly, and many works of art depict her along with a single butterfly. There is a famous Roman sculpture of a butterfly flying up from the mouth of a recently deceased hero, a visual representation of the belief that on its journey to the next world, the transformed human soul departed from the mouth.

Curiously enough, there are not many butterfly stories in British folklore. There are superstitions, of course. It is widely believed to be unlucky to kill white butterflies, apart from in Devon, where it is believed that if you kill the first white butterfly of the year that you see you will have good luck from then on. Killing white butterflies was illegal in Ireland up until the 1600s – it was believed that if you killed one, you were killing the innocent soul of a deceased, unbaptized child. In some northern English counties, it is said that if you cup a butterfly in your palms and whisper to it your secret wishes, the gently released butterfly will carry them away to the Fae, and your wishes will most certainly be granted. The 'eyes' on butterfly wings are said to be the eyes of God, spying on human sins and indiscretions.

If a butterfly lands on your shoulder at night, or three happen to chance upon your shoulder by day, you are believed to be doomed and might as well write out your last will and testament there and then.

If a red butterfly lands upon you, important good news is on the way. This also indicates good luck in passion and affairs of the heart – a love letter may well be on its way. Other colours and circumstances indicated by butterfly landings on a person:

Orange – joy is imminent; you will have an unexpected visitor or invitation.

Yellow – it will be a sunny summer for you, with much fun and the potential for a new life.

Green – success in business or property ventures.

Blue – protection against vindictive persons and good luck, with a wish being granted.

Black – death or renewal – black butterflies are said to be the unhappy souls of those that cannot yet move on to an after-life. They are also believed to indicate that thunderstorms are brewing.

If a butterfly settles on or near a laid-out corpse, the dead person will enjoy eternal happiness in the afterlife. Landing on a uniformed sailor heading for his ship, the butterfly brings ill-luck – the sailor will possibly perish on his next sea voyage
.

Some Moth and Caterpillar Lore

The poor cousin of the butterfly, moths seem slightly sinister as they tend to emerge as darkness falls, and they are associated with the destruction of clothing and fabrics. They represent the slow perishing of things that we cherish, and of course, attracted to naked flames, they have become linked to the notion of self-destruction and suicide. The Luna Moth, however, is linked to patterns of rebirth, regeneration and the feminine creative energies of the moon. They are thought to be like artists – creative, light seeking but sometimes self-neglectful and potentially destructive.

A caterpillar is, of course, a butterfly in the making. The great naturalist and writer, Charles Darwin, saw in the life cycle of the butterfly the journey of the human soul. The caterpillar phase is representative of the struggles, work and tribulations of life; the pupa phase represents death and transformation; the final butterfly stage is the emergence of the transformed, winged soul into a glorious after-life. There are some fantastical and magical butterfly stories to seek out and consider from beyond the British Isles, if any reader is so inclined. The fable by Aesop, The Butterfly and The Rose, with its message about vanity and infidelity, is worth consideration. The wonderful tale 'The Wings of The Butterfly', a magical adventure tale sourced from the Tukuna tribe in the upper Amazon, is worth reading, and could in fact be representative of a butterfly tale from any culture world-wide.

Centipedes – Chilopoda

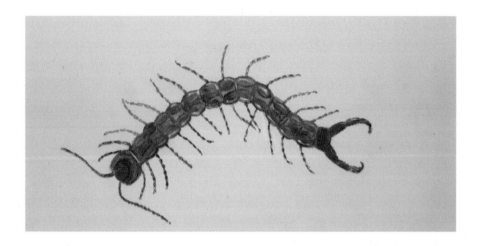

A centipede joke:

Q. *What goes ninety-nine, clunk, ninety-nine clunk, ninety-nine clunk?*

Centipedes, those of the hundred feet, are a most beautiful looking insect. Pretty as they might be, these nocturnal, multi-segmented, elongated arthropods are rather deadly. World-wide, there are over 8000 species of centipede, and not one of them actually has 100 legs. The leg numbers vary from 30 to 354, and through some quirk of nature the pairs on any species always come in odd numbers so the total never adds up to 100.

Centipedes are mainly carnivorous, feeding on other insects, especially slugs, small spiders, flies and worms. Surprisingly, they can live for up to six years, so for those inclined, they make great insect pets. However, they do have a painful venomous bite, something that feels like a bee sting, but this is not usually lethal or harmful to humans.

If you kill a centipede with your bare hands it is meant to bring good luck – though not to the centipede. If you choose to try this, be very careful as there are stories about people being bitten on the hand then dying an agonising death over the next two days or, perhaps even worse, the skin rotting and dropping off around the bite and never regrowing, the skin-rot gradually spreading from the hand over the entire body.

In China, large centipedes are eagerly consumed as street-food in some large cities, the delicacy usually deep fried or served on skewers.

There are many alleged accounts of centipedes (and their close cousins, millipedes) lodging in the nose sinuses and ear canals of animals, including humans. Once lodged and nested in the ear, their scritching and scratching noises as they go about their business (breeding, feeding, laying eggs and the like), torments the host, prevents them from sleeping and is known to have led to people committing suicide through the creature's unintentional torture. As gruesome and wonderful as this sounds, it is said to be quite false and pure conjecture. Best leave them alone though, just in case.

The Centipede Cleansing Cure

Crushed, dried then powdered centipedes are known to dissipate toxins and poisons from the human body. The powder is especially good for kidney and liver ailments. The centipede dust is sprinkled in a posset of warm milk, honey and powdered cinnamon and imbibed at leisure. Three teaspoons of powdered centipede in three cups of the mixture a day over three days is the recommended dose. This cure however is not recommended for pregnant or lactating women due to potentially strong anti-toxins in the mixture.

Traditional medicine from all around the world features 'centipede cures', with the venom being particularly prized. Cures for ailments created used from this wonderful little insect include:

Stroke induced hemiplegia, epilepsy, apoplexy and other types of fits, tetanus, whooping cough, burns, tuberculosis, arthritis, tumours and myocutaneous disease. Indeed, is there any ailment this astounding creature cannot cure? Research of use of the venom in helping epilepsy is currently ongoing as is highly likely to result in a cure for this illness.

There is an ancient belief in Kent, entrenched around the Canterbury area, that centipedes destroy children's teeth. If a child is found chewing or sucking a centipede (well, they can grow up to 8 inches long – or up to 12 inches long in the Amazon jungle - and they do look quite sweet and crunchy) the creature must be killed immediately, the mouth scrubbed and rinsed out, and the teeth counted. It is believed that centipedes steal the child's teeth, or somehow cause them to rot, which can result in the child's untimely death from gum infection. While most of the children in the UK pop a dropped-out tooth under their pillow expecting the Tooth Fairy to exchange it for good money, in Canterbury the children expect the Tooth Centipede to whisk away the tooth. Their canny parents have trained them to expect nothing but a ten pence coin in return for their gob loss.

Robin Hood and The Gigantic Centipede

There is a North Yorkshire myth about a gigantic man-eating centipede that lived in the hills around Robin Hood's Bay. On the full moon, it used to descend into the towns and villages, invariably snatching up humans, usually children, and usually naughty ones at that. It was said to wear a protective cloak of chain mail to protect it from the spears, arrows and swords of those that tried to dispatch it. In the moonlight this cloak looked something like a giant cardigan, and the hideous creature became known as Oh-My-Cardi. Some folklorists dispute this name, however, and think the locals picked up the name from Japanese visitors at the time, who had a similar creature back in their own country known as Omakade. The visitors informed the locals that the hideous Omakade had been destroyed by one of their heroes, Tawara Toda Hidesato (also known as 'Rice Bag Toda'), a master archer and bowman, who dispatched the hundred-legged fiend with an arrow laced with his own spit – apparently human spittle is a highly toxic substance to centipedes.

On the next full moon, the locals around Robin Hood's Bay called in their own master archer, Robin Hood, to try and kill the creature once and for all. Robin, sitting on Little John's shoulders for greater height, fired off several arrows at the creature, going for the eyes, but they just bounced off without leaving a single mark. Robin was soon down to his last arrow.
 'Spit on it!' yelled Little John. 'Spit on it! Didn't you listen to the story?' So, Robin hawked and grebbed and spat all over the iron head of his last arrow. The monster was almost upon them, but he managed to fire off the last arrow. It pierced the creature's chain mail cardigan and lodged in its heart, killing it instantly.

Everybody was saved. Robin Hood and Little John were great heroes. And for a while after, the little coastal town where the monster was slain was known as Little John's Bay. But as time went on and the star of Robin's ascended in stories and folklore, the mayor and councilors knew a good move when they saw one. The town was discretely re-named Robin Hood's Bay. This proved to be a good move as tourists still flock there to this day.

A) A centipede with a wooden leg.

Cockroaches – Blattodea

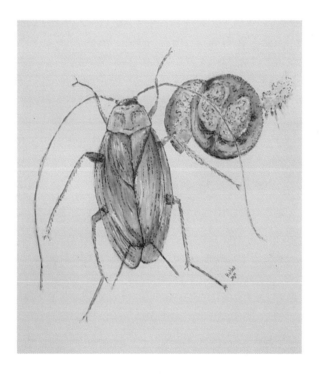

'La cucaracha, la cucaracha
Ya nopuede caminar,
Porque no tiene, porque le falta,
Mariguana que fumar…'

circa 1910 – Mexican Revolutionary anthem.

Cockroaches do not bite. They do not smoke either, although they are said to be fond of beer. In fact, they are quite decent, fabulous and amazing creatures, despite being somewhat repellent looking and for some reason quite loathsome to most humans. They are symbolically associated with 'perseverance and survival'. As a species they have existed on this planet for 300 million years. Our modern ancestors only evolved about 200 000 years ago. So, between themselves, they probably know a thing or two more than us about survival.

Cockroaches will eat anything, even metal and other cockroaches. Apparently, they can survive and thrive quite happily on the glue on the back of postage stamps. Although associated with filth, they will invade a sparkling clean home as nonchalantly as a dirty one. They have no respect for disinfectant or vacuum cleaners. According to legend, they can happily survive for months without food and weeks without water. Astoundingly, a cockroach can hold its breath underwater for over 40 minutes and can live without a head for up to a week. In China they are reverentially referred to as 'The Little Mighty One' due to the fact that they can regenerate limbs and can live without a head for over a week. Yes, we are aware some of you might not quite believe that – but the videos are out there!

Worldwide, there are 4500 different species of cockroach, although only 30 are regarded as 'pests'. There are only 3 species native to The British Isles, but these do not normally come into homes. Abroad in hot climates, they are 'ten a penny', especially around damp and cool, interior areas, like the shower or bathroom. I have only ever seen one live specimen in the UK, when I was a younger child - a huge red one, as big as a double-decker bus! Or so it seemed at the time. In the swimming pool changing rooms. Just scuttling along. The memory still makes me shudder.

Cockroaches and Medicine

Cockroaches have many medicinal uses. Crushed and powdered then ground into garlic laced olive oil, they can be used as a cure for earache. In China, twice fried cockroaches are renowned as a health benefit and tasty snack, a dish that is good for combating indigestion. The Romans in York and those stationed in the-back-of-beyond at Hadrian's wall, used cockroaches dried and crushed into pig fat as a rub-on cure for insect stings and midge bites. In certain parts of Yorkshire, folk infested with fleas or mites are still known to rub 'Cockroach Dripping' over their bodies after bathing or before bedtime. In Bristol, using a Creole recipe brought over from the Caribbean, cockroach tea was an old remedy for tetanus and anxiety, and in certain notorious corner shops it can still be purchased, under the counter, in brown paper bags.
In Madagascar and Cuba, cockroaches are kept as pets by many people. The 'green banana cockroach' is favoured in Cuba, while the huge, noisy, shriek emitting cutie, also known as The Hissing Cockroach, is favoured in Madagascar.

Of course, *'the song'* has to be mentioned and referenced in any folk lore piece about cockroaches. Everybody knows it, even though they might think that they do not. The Mexican Revolutionary song about the resilient cockroach that is hobbling along out of kilter after losing its leg. And the numerous variants on the theme, including the one about the marijuana smoking cockroach that is too smashed to walk home. And now, of course, you will have to find it and play it and have an irresistible sunny Latin shimmy. La Cucaracha! Apologies for that little earworm.

Daddy Long-Legs - Pholcidae /Tipulidae

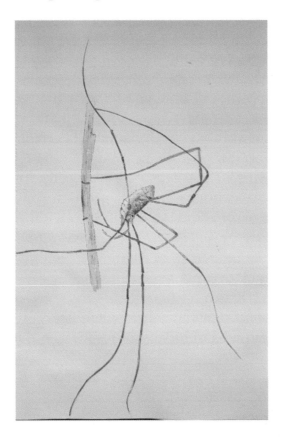

Also known as: the marbled cellar spider, carpenter spider, vibrating spider, gyrating spider, long daddy, skull spider, harvestmen.

Perhaps, along with woodlice and earwigs, Daddy-Long-Legs are one of the creepiest creepy-crawlies, and they certainly arouse fear, revulsion and a full shudder amongst the hardest of men! Women, of course, deal with them practically, throwing them out into the night (with their bare hands!). Children tend to avoid them as they are silent and creepy, although the naughtier, crueler ones have been known to pull off a few of the spindly legs, just to see what happens. They are related to spiders and, technically speaking, are arachnids, but they do not spin webs. Unlike spiders they only have 2 eyes, not eight, and their body is not divided into segments.

There is a total myth (perhaps perpetrated by cowering men) that the daddy-long-legs is amongst the most venomous spiders in the world and that a bite can kill – but this is actually total nonsense. Their tiny fangs are not even big enough to pierce human skin, let alone inject lethal venom. In fact, they do not possess venom glands at all, and there is some scientific debate as to whether they even have fangs. They do have a form of chemical defence, secreting droplets of a milky white liquid through their body that apparently tastes vile and repels predators. Apparently, if eaten they are not to be very tasty, with a bitter, metallic after-taste, and unlike several other insects in these islands, they are not recommended as a snack or food source. Mainly vegetarians, they feed as scavengers, eating dead organic matter and, if the opportunity rises, a treat of injured or dying insects.

Some Daddy long-legs lore

Every daddy-long-legs or harvestman own a scythe, and they are happy to help farmers mow the hay and reap in the harvest. Thus, killing a daddy long-legs is sure to bring bad luck. If you do kill a daddy-long-legs if will almost certainly rain the following day, which is not fortuitous if attempting to harvest the wheat and barley. Seeing a daddy long legs in the evening is a good sign, foretelling good fortune and happiness in the coming days. Herdsmen in the northern counties used to use harvestmen to locate lost or straying cattle. If one was picked up and held by seven of its eight legs, the eight leg would point and wave in the direction of the wayward stock.

They are said to be able to discard of their legs at will, and can regenerate lost legs when they molt, shedding their exoskeleton as they progress through their life. It must be said, that even as insects go, Daddy-Long-Legs are pretty weird! They breathe through spiral fissures positioned at the tops of their legs. Their legs are spiny and hairy and, most bizarrely of all, they nibble upon the hairs of each other's legs for pleasure.

Overall, despite their silent, meandering creepishness, these fragile creatures are benign and sociable insects, who like to gather in groups for leg-nibbling and collective protection. They do not bite, make a mess or poison anything. They have been known to have 'staring competitions', and this seems to be something of a sport when they do collect together. Rival daddy-long-legs will square up an inch or so apart, and will stare into each other's eyes, apparently seeing which of them can go the longest without blinking. The loser (first blinker) will scuttle aside, with a fresh challenger shuffling up to take its place. Such competitions have been known to go on for several hours, and even days, with the 'sporting event' only breaking up when feeding is necessary, or predators are approaching.

If you are an attentive or critical reader, you will have noticed that daddy-long-legs has been presented in a variety of hyphenated and spelled forms in this piece. The reason for this is that there is no officially correct spelling or hyphenation of the word/words in the English language. So, we thought that we would let you decide. Daddy Long Legs. Daddy-long Legs. Or Daddy-long-legs?

Dragonflies – Odonata

Also known as: *Horse-stinger. Devil's Darning needle. Eye-poker. Eye-snatcher. Ear-cutter. Adder's Servant. Snake Doctor. Head-darter. Soul-hawk. Soul-chases. Hawker. Skimmer. Damselfly.*

The Dragonfly
Today I saw a dragonfly
Come from the wells where he did lie.
An inner impulse rent the veil
Of his old husk: from head to tail
Came out clear plates of sapphire mail.
He dries his wings: like gauze they grew;
Thro' crofts and pastures wet with dew
A living flash of light he flew.

Alfred, Lord Tennyson, from The Two Voices, 1833

They can hover. They can fly backwards. They are one of the fastest flying insects on the planet, reaching speeds of over 30 miles per hour. They are some of the most colourful insects in the world and come in a dazzling array of colours, including iridescent blues, fluorescent greens and yellows, psychedelic reds and subtle lilacs. Their large, multi-eyed compound eyes enable them to see in all directions simultaneously, continually looking out for food and predators. They have large, fearsome jaws, hence their Greek name, Odonta, which means 'tooth'. Amazing, beautiful, awe-inspiring creatures – yet there seems to be little folklore associated with them in the British Isles. Despite their beauty, throughout Europe they are often viewed as sinister things, associated with evil, injury, snakes and the Devil, as indicated by the localised names for them printed above. Although ferocious predators, helpfully devouring gnats and mosquitos amongst other things (including butterflies and smaller dragonflies), often holding and eating them as they fly, they rarely bite people, and even when they do, their bite is seldom fatal.

Some Dragonfly Lore

If a dragonfly lands on your head, it is meant to be a sign of good luck. In Wales, where the insect is known as an 'adder's servant', it was believed that dragonflies worked closely with snakes to pester humans and share food sources. If a snake was injured, the dragonfly would help it, stitching back together any wounds and helping to heal its friend. This lore is also believed in parts of the USA, where dragonflies are called 'snake doctors', this belief having probably been brought over to the America's by immigrant settlers from Wales.

On a more positive side, dragonfly sightings are said to indicate a positive change or new beginning, as well as being recognised as a symbol of living in the moment, enjoying to the full the 'here and now', and taking full advantage of the beauty and transience of life. It is with these more positive elements in mind that image is often used in beautiful items of jewellery, especially brooches, hairpieces and hatpins.

In Somerset it is believed that it is inadvisable to fall asleep outdoors in the summer months, especially after a touch of scrumpy - fall asleep near a pond or ditch at night and a dragonfly (or a 'devil's darning needle'), would almost certainly stitch together your fingers and toes. Other widespread beliefs about the sewing abilities of dragonflies are:

They will stitch the wounds of injured snakes together.

They will sew shut the eyes of naughty children who sneak outdoors at night.

They will sew shut the mouths of children who are rude, or use swear words.

On the full moon they will sew up the mouths of people who nag, natter or complain too much -and especially the mouths of nagging middle-aged men.

Dragonflies as food – curried or barbequed?

Like any insect, dragonflies as water-based larvae or as flying adults, are a viable source of protein, although the speedy, flying adults are said to be quite difficult to catch. Any survivalist, back-packer or serious entomophagist worth their salt would have them marked as a readily available food. Raw, fresh or dried, dragonfly meat will fend off starvation, and as a staple can be used to replace any of the main protein sources in any of the recipes in this book. In Indonesia, adult dragonflies are considered a delicacy. Children hunt them in the rice fields using sticky, sap-smeared bamboo poles. They remove the wings from their catch, pierce them onto a wooden skewer then lightly roast them to make a tasty snack. Any surplus bodies are taken home for the family, where they are coated in spiced oil then grilled, barbeque-style, over charcoal, or deep-fried in coconut oil with fresh vegetables, herbs, spices, ginger, chilies, and garlic. Chicken, beef, tofu or fresh snake can be used in place of dragonflies.

It is difficult not to be amazed by these wonderful, flickering bright and ephemeral creatures when spotting them in the wild. Dedicated dragonfly spotters are technically known as 'odanists', to go spotting them is to go 'oding', the word rooted from the Latin scientific order classification 'Odanata'. For further information you might look up or contact The British Dragonfly Society, who work to conserve dragonflies and their natural wetland habitats.

Earwigs – Dermaptera

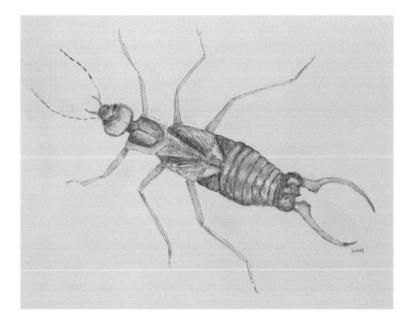

Also known as: ear-wriggler, earworm, ear-turner, battle-twig, wonder-mum.

Earwigs in literature:

'A big fat earwig is very tasty,' Grandma said, licking her lips. 'But you've got to be very quick, my dear.'

Roald Dahl, 'George's Marvelous Medicine' –
(said as his atrocious Grandma encourages George to eat live earwigs from unwashed celery).

Earwigs in everyday life

Every child's nightmare insect. They are alleged to sneakily crawl into the inner ear to lay their eggs into warm moistness there. The hatched baby insects then bore onward into the brain for easy food, causing paralysis, agony and madness. This, of course, is not true – but the legend makes them high up there on the loathsome creepy-crawly scale. They are actually mainly vegetarian, although they will eat smaller insects and feed on carrion – i.e. dead bodies – if the opportunity arises.

There are about 2,000 species in 12 families and are one of the smaller insect orders, although only 4 types are found in the British Isles. Earwigs have a pair of nasty looking pincers on their rear abdomen, hence their ferocious reputation. The males and females have different shaped pincers – curved ones on males, straight ones on females. They can pinch and cling onto your finger with these forceps, but they won't hurt much, and do not inject venom with them, nor do they bite or sting humans. The fierce looking pincers are mainly used to catch smaller insect prey, to fend of predators, and they are vital in this insect's elaborate mating rituals.
 Although rarely seen flying, earwigs do have delicate short wings which are folded beneath their bodies, known as "skin wings". Earwigs are found all over the planet and thrive on all continents except Antarctica. They are nocturnal creatures and don't like to be seen, usually hiding away in cracks, crevices and tubular hollows in the hours of daylight.

Earwig Sex Life

It is said that earwigs tap each other's bellies then nibble each other's extended pincers while preparing to mate -something also known also known as 'wiggie foreplay'. Male earwigs have supersized genitalia, called virga. In some species, the rod-like virga is as long as the male's body length, and twice as long as the female. When the male extracts the virga, which has a brim shaped penis tip, it cleans out sperm from other males that have previously mated with the female, hence increasing his chance of successful procreation. Surprisingly perhaps, female earwigs are very maternal. They lick their hatched eggs to keep them clean and fungi free then look after their newly young – known as 'nymphs' - until they are able to thrive independently.

Earwigs as food

Can you eat earwigs? Of course you can, if so inclined, or in need in dire circumstances. Earwigs are said to be quite tasty - ma cross between chicken and shrimp. Prepare them the same as termites or cockroaches. A couple of tactics for gathering them come from gardeners who are not over fond of these little creatures, even though they help the garden to be clear of aphids. Fill low-sided tubs (the plastic food storage ones are ideal) with a half inch of vegetable oil and place them on the ground near piles of logs or other mounds of garden debris. The earwigs will pour in and baste themselves as they drown – all ready for a lightly fried supper-time snack. A sprinkle of parmesan cheese and a glass of red wine helps them down.

Fleas – Siphonaptera

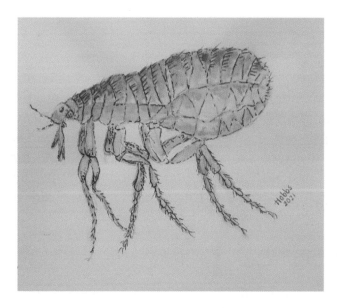

Surprisingly, several 'great' poets have been inspired by fleas. Here is a verse the from Jonathan Swift's long satirical poem "On Poetry: a Rhapsody" (1733):

The vermin only teaze and pinch
Their foes superior by an inch.
So, naturalists observe, a flea
Has smaller fleas that on him prey;
And these have smaller still to bite 'em,
And so proceed ad infinitum.
Thus every poet, in his kind,
Is bit by him that comes behind.

And of course:

From 'The Flea' – John Donne
'Mark but this flea and mark in this,
How little that which thou deniest me is;
It sucked me first, and now sucks thee,
And in this flea our two bloods mingled be;

Thou know'st that this cannot be said
A sin, nor shame, nor loss of maidenhead,
Yet this enjoys before it woo,
And pampered swells with one blood made of two,
And this, alas, is more than we would do.'

Possibly one of the best (or worst?) bedside, chat-up lines ever?

Humans, as well as animals, have a long, close and intimate relationship with fleas. The human flea – also known as the house flea – is quite rare on the inhabitants of the British Isles these days, although the cat flea (which also infests dogs) is still very common and will happily take a bite and suck on a handy passing human host. A tiny, external parasite, light-hating that lives by consuming blood, there are over 2500 species of this vampiric creature on the planet. Flat and wingless, they have strong claws to help prevent them being dislodged by their itchy host, and jaws which have evolved for the sole purpose of sucking blood. They are endowed with intricate, quite amazing legs adapted and structured for astounding feats of leaping. With their legs, which become like taut bows pulled ready to unleash an arrow, they are able to leap relatively astounding distances. Most fleas are capable of jumping 50 to 80 times longer or higher than their own body length. So, if a flea was a six-foot-tall human, it would be able to leap at least 300 feet into the air or along the street in one go. The current word record for long jumping for humans is a paltry 30 feet.

Fleas are also renowned for having disproportionately large penises, which can extend to two and half times their bodily length. Back to the human comparison, this would equate a fifteen-foot-long penis for the average male. That would possibly make day-to-day life quite difficult.

Each flea species has evolved as a specialist with respect to its host animal or bird species and, other than cat fleas, tend to stick to their favoured food-source. They have evolved sideways flat and wingless so that they can easily weave and move through the body hair or feathers of their blood-filled host.

Fleas and Death

Fleas have caused quite a few problems for human mortality rates in the past and may still do so in the future. Xenopsylla Cheopis, better known as the oriental rat flea, carries a bacterium known as Yersina Pestis. That all sounds very grand, but this was, and still is, the cause of bubonic plague. This virulent plague with its horrific symptoms was passed onto humans via rodents such as the black rat, which were infected with the plague by flea bites. Scientists today believe that the plague originated in the far-east, most likely in China, working its way west with traders along the ancient Silk Road. The Plague of Justinian between 541 and 549 AD almost wiped out the Roman empire, especially in its eastern provinces, with up to 10 000 deaths per day for months on end recoded in Constantinople at its peak. Another terrible outbreak, known infamously as The Black Death, 1346 to 1353, was the most fatal pandemic ever recorded in human history, wiping out an estimated 60% of the European population alone (killing at least one hundred million people). Fleas literally changed the course of human history. Outbreaks of bubonic plague reoccurred around the world on a regular basis until the Victorian era, and localised outbreaks still regularly occur to this day.

Rather tragically, humans being humans, flea transmitted diseases have been experimented with and used in biological warfare. Bubonic plague was used in biological weapon attacks against China by the Japanese in the second world war. Bombs were loaded with plague infected fleas hidden in sand, wheat corn and scraps of cotton cloth, then dropped in the district of Kaimingjie, in the Zhejiang province. The attacks caused an outbreak of plague that resulted in hundreds of deaths and massive social disruption.

Flea Circuses

In the past as far back as the 1500s performing fleas were a popular circus sideshow and country fair attraction. Fleas were attached to miniature carts, tightropes, trapezes and other items after being trained to perform astounding feats and acrobatic acts of marvellous skill and dexterity.

Originally the early flea performances were set up by watchmakers who were, the entertaining show aside, demonstrating their intricate gold wire and metalworking skills. Some flea circuses persisted in very small venues in the United States as late as the 1960s. A flea circus in Manchester was still operating in the 1970s. One common act in flea circuses was the 'flea music band'. Fleas were glued to the base of a metallic flea circus disc and tiny musical instruments were glued to their bodies. When the base was cunningly heated from beneath, the fleas tried to escape but because they were glued fast in their frantic movements it appeared as though they were actually playing their instruments. Witnessing one such performance a young lad from Liverpool, Paul McCartney, was inspired to take up the guitar and form his own musical band, 'The Fleas'. However, they were re-named after another common insect when their management team decided that 'The Fleas' lacked sufficient commercial potential as a musical band name. The new band, The Beatles, went on to do quite well.

Fleas - Culinary Dishes and Medicinal Cures

There are no known medicinal cures or culinary dishes associated with fleas. Potentially containing disease and toxins after feasting on fresh blood, it is not advisable to cook or eat them, unless absolutely necessary.

Flies – Diptera

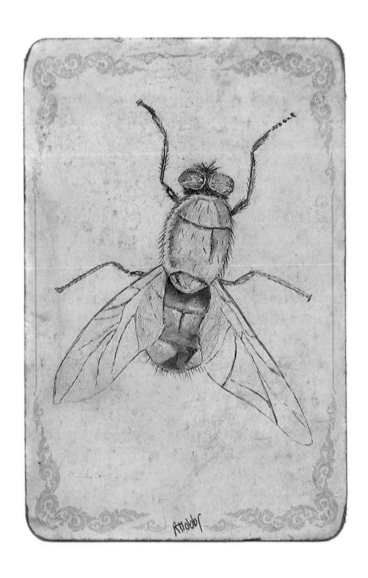

They bite, they sting, they suck blood, transmit diseases, walk on faeces and then on our food and are just generally annoying. No, not children – flies! Possibly the most reviled and disliked insect in the world, troublesome throughout the world from pole to pole, surviving and breeding prolifically in every possible environment. Unlike most flying insects, they use only a single pair of wings to fly, their 'back wings' having evolved into complex rotating paddles which enable them to perform advanced, high-speed aerobatics. It is estimated that there are over a million different species of fly on the planet but only 150 000 species formally described including crane flies, hover flies, horse flies and of course the ever-annoying houseflies and blue bottles. They have mobile heads with a pair of large compound, multi-lensed eyes along with claws and pads on their feet which enable them to cling effortlessly to smooth horizontal and vertical surfaces such as ceilings and windows. No wonder it is so difficult to swat them with a rolled-up newspaper.

It is well known that some flies suck up rotting liquid food and then regurgitate it before re-eating the expelled liquid matter. That is to say, they eat their own vomit. Any moving image media version of 'The Fly', including the wonderful Simpson's version, dwells on this quaint dietary feature. Just for useful party banter, the technical term for this table habit is *'bubbling'*.

Some Positive things About Flies

Flies are great plant pollinators, second only to bees. Some scientists believe that they were the planet's first pollinating creatures and enabled plants to reproduce, adapt and survive. The world as we know it now could never have existed without these early flies, and the chances of the human species evolving would have been minimal.

Flies have medicinal uses. Fly larvae (maggots), particularly those of the green bottle, have long been used to help heal burns and open wounds. The helpful maggots eat the rotting tissue in the wounds - the necrotic, infected tissue - but leave the healthy tissue alone, a useful healing process known as *debridement* – the removal of debris. Fruit flies - *drosophila* – have been essential to medical, biological and genetic research since the twentieth century. As bizarre as it might seem, the relationship between human genes and fruit fly genes is very close. Seventy five percent of disease-causing genes in humans are also found in the humble fruit fly, hence their usefulness in medical research.

There is a belief and practise in the beneficial use of drinking 'fly water'. As flies are, by their filthy nature, covered in bacteria, viruses, disease spores and pathogenic microbes, some believe that by dipping or soaking them in a liquid then drinking the filtered, fly-free liquid many ailments, diseases and afflictions can be cured or averted – a sort of multi-purpose vaccination tonic.

Flies, Legends, Folklore and Mythology

Flies have a symbolic and mythic history in many cultures around the world, but there are not so many stories related to them in The British Isles. Aesop had a few fables about them of course – The Fly and The Mule and The Fly on The Chariot Wheel, where the tiny creatures are rather full of their own self-worth and importance. The demonic fly, Beelzebub, is important in Christian mythology. He was a deity of the Philistines, ancient enemies of the Israelites, linked to the god Baal, to whom child sacrifices were offered as a matter of course. Biblically, he is one of the so-called Seven Princes of Hell and is known as The Lord of The Flies. Intimately connected with the Christian concept of Satan and Lucifer, some theologians believe that Satan and Beelzebub are in fact one and the same. Any lover of literature will know of the important role Beelzebub plays in Christopher Marlowe's great English play, 'Doctor Faustus'. And, of course, will have read the novel, 'The Lord of The Flies' by William Golding. On the literary front though, there is one hugely important poem featuring a spider and a hapless fly, that it would be criminal to leave out of a book about insect folklore. We refer to *The Spider and The Fly* by Mary Howitt. Creepy and sinister until the brutal end, we were only going to use a quote from it here but have decided that it would be neglectful not to print it in its entirety. Best read out loud. Preferably to an audience of small, nervous children.

The Spider and The Fly 'Will you walk into my parlour?'
said a spider to a fly;
' 'Tis the prettiest little parlour that ever you did spy.
The way into my parlour is up a winding stair,
And I have many pretty things to shew when you are there.'
'Oh no, no!' said the little fly, 'to ask me is in vain,
For who goes up your winding stair can ne'er come down
again.'

'I'm sure you must be weary, with soaring up so high,
Will you rest upon my little bed?' said the spider to the fly.
'There are pretty curtains drawn around, the sheets are fine
and thin;
And if you like to rest awhile, I'll snugly tuck you in.'
'Oh no, no!' said the little fly, 'for I've often heard it said,
They never, never wake again, who sleep upon your bed!'

Said the cunning spider to the fly, 'Dear friend, what shall I
do,
To prove the warm affection I've always felt for you?
I have, within my pantry, good store of all that's nice;
I'm sure you're very welcome — will you please to take a slice?'
'Oh no, no!' said the little fly, 'kind sir, that cannot be,
I've heard what's in your pantry, and I do not wish to see.'

'Sweet creature!' said the spider, 'you're witty and you're
wise.
How handsome are your gauzy wings, how brilliant are your
eyes!
I have a little looking-glass upon my parlour shelf,
If you'll step in one moment, dear, you shall behold yourself.'
'I thank you, gentle sir,' she said, 'for what you're pleased to
say,
And bidding you good morning now, I'll call another day.'

The spider turned him round about, and went into his den,

For well he knew, the silly fly would soon come back again:
So he wove a subtle web, in a little corner, sly,
And set his table ready, to dine upon the fly.
Then he went out to his door again, and merrily did sing,
'Come hither, hither, pretty fly, with the pearl and silver wing;
Your robes are green and purple---there's a crest upon your
head;
Your eyes are like the diamond bright, but mine are dull as
lead.'

Alas, alas! how very soon this silly little fly,
Hearing his wily, flattering words, came slowly flitting by;
With buzzing wings she hung aloft, then near and nearer
drew,
Thinking only of her brilliant eyes, and green and purple
hue:—
Thinking only of her crested head, poor foolish thing!—At last
Up jumped the cunning spider, and fiercely held her fast.

He dragged her up his winding stair, into his dismal den,
Within his little parlour—but she ne'er came out again!
—And now, dear little children, who may this story read,
To idle, silly, flattering words, I pray you ne'er give heed:
Unto an evil counsellor, close heart, and ear, and eye,
And take a lesson from this tale, of the Spider and the Fly.

Glow Worms – lampyridae

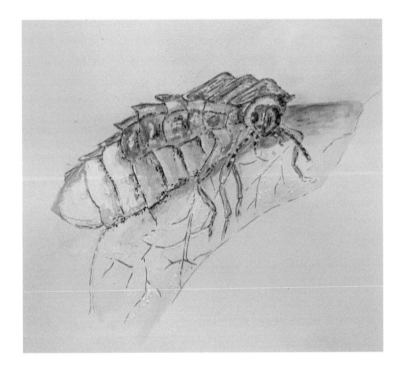

AKA fire flies, lightning bugs, goblin lights, will-o-the-wisp, the love torch, glow-bard.

Twinkling away in gardens, forests, hedgerows and marshlands, the female members of this insect family glow for a very simple reason – to attract mates. Their ability to shine is beautifully termed *bioluminescence*. Or in English, living creature light. The males do not have the ability to glow and shine, and in fact they are relatively rather ugly. Imagine a woodlouse with wings. Of course, they are not worms at all, but a variety of beetle. Glow worms are quite fierce predators, who will eat slugs, snails and any smaller insects. They are said to be able to eat snails twenty times their own size by injecting them with a paralysing neurotoxin which dissolves the living snail's body. They siphon off and suck up the liquid as the snail is dying. Hopefully, they will not mutate do to gigantic proportions and get a taste for human juices. When the ground-hugging, flightless female has mated her ability to glow ceases and then, like her mate, is a very ordinary looking small beetle.

British glow worm Folklore

It is said that ancient Britons used to collect up glow worms and use them to provide lights in their huts and cave dwellings. They also used them to mark out safe pathways in the bogs and fens of Cambridgeshire and Norfolk. They became associated with the rather sinister folk figure of will-o'- the wisp', a gaseous sprite who used to entice travellers to their doom in the bogs and wetlands, leading them to quicksand rather than the safe path. Fairies are also said to collect glow worms in glass jars to light up their caverns and hollows.

The 'glow bard's' seasonal display of illumination was said to herald the start of the hay harvest and indicated the ripeness of the barley. In modern times, they have been used as emergency bicycle lamps and used as floats by canny fishermen for night-fishing.

Glow worms are popular in Japanese, Chinese and Persian medicine. In Persia, they were collected, crushed, mixed with the attar of roses and dripped into the ear to prevent weeping wax and to cure ear infections.

In Suffolk, young maidens would weave them into their hair for night-decoration and to lure the boys, whereas the boys would tie them on a thread around their boots to light up the fen paths at night.

Grasshoppers – Orthoptera

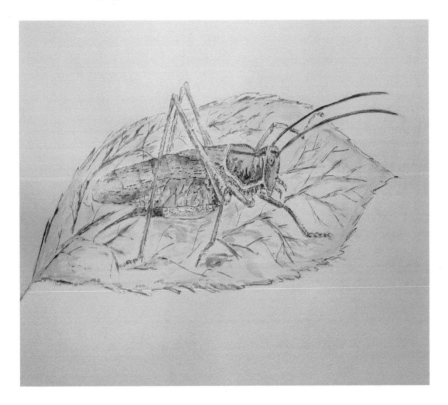

In the fable of Aesop, the grasshopper is a somewhat reckless, pleasure-seeking insect. While the do-gooder ant works hard, collects and stores food and labours away all summer long, the grasshopper sings, dances and has a good time. Come winter, of course, the feckless fellow has no food while the ant has its hoarded store. Starving, the grasshopper begs for some food from the ant. There could have been a happier ending to this tale, but the ant refuses to give the starving cricket any charity. The ant rebukes the grasshopper and says, 'You sang and danced all summer. Now sing and dance through the winter.'

The grasshopper starves to death.

The moral: work hard and save in youth or die in old age in poverty.

Some Differences Between Grasshoppers and Crickets

Size is the most significant difference between the two insects. An adult grasshopper is larger than an adult cricket. In terms of colour, the average grasshopper is green while the crickets are black or brown. Grasshoppers are among one of the most ancient living group of chewing herbivorous insects, dating back to the early Triassic era around 250 million years ago. Grasshoppers and crickets make sounds in one of two ways – stridulation or crepitation. Like their cricket cousins, grasshoppers produce sounds to attract mates or protect territory. Grasshoppers can be identified by their unique songs, which differ slightly from species to species. They make sounds by rubbing their forelegs against their wings, while crickets rub their wings together. Grasshoppers are diurnal (active during the day). Crickets are nocturnal (active during the night). Grasshoppers only eat plants, while crickets are omnivorous – they will eat plants, seeds other animals and insects – including grasshoppers!

Grasshopper Folklore and Superstitions

Grasshoppers and crickets in the home are said to be beneficial and signs of good luck the world over. They are the guardians of the home and the young. Who can forget 'Jimmy Cricket', the sidekick and guardian of the hapless Pinocchio. Traditionally, a cricket was kept by the fireplace of a house to bring good luck and protection against dangers. Apparently, they make good and loyal pets. There is an obscure story by Charles Dickens, 'The Cricket in the Hearth', which explores this notion and tradition, well worth a read, but far too long to include here.

Cicadas are technically a different species of insect even though they look very similar to grasshoppers and crickets. Common in Europe and warmer climates, they are very rare, if not extinct now, in the British Isles. Only one species has actually been identified and recorded, in The New Forest down in Hampshire. Unfortunately, none of these have been heard or sighted in over fifteen years, but hopefully a few little groups survive and cling on.

Being mainly a European insect, far away over the English Channel, there are myths and legends associated with them, particularly in Greek literature. A handsome, strapping and virile fellow, Tithonus, is said to have been the first Cicada. He was a mortal but was having a passionate affair with the goddess Eos. She wanted to live with forever with him, such was his prowess, so begged and pleaded with Zeus, chief God, to grant him eternal life. Eventually Zeus gave into her pleadings and met with her request. There was a slight oversight in the plan, however. Tithonus did have eternal life, but not eternal youth. He aged through time and grew so old, shrunken and shriveled that eventually he turned into the first Cicada. It is not recorded whether Eos remained faithfully with him as his lover, but there are rumours that she moved on to more virile mortal lovers as he aged over fifty and started to wither
.

Grasshoppers and crickets as food

Incredible as it might seem, there are many grasshopper dishes available. These include grasshopper pie, grasshopper cheesecake, grasshopper cake and even a grasshopper cocktail drink. It must be admitted that these do not all contain actual grasshoppers. However, plucked, cleaned and the intestines removed, they are a serious source of protein and are eaten all over the world. Here is a quick and easy dish, but make sure you wash and clean the 'meat' first, as sometimes they contain worms and other parasites.

Ingredients

> Three cupped handfuls of grasshoppers (or crickets).

> A splash of olive oil or heated, unsalted butter.

Sprinkling of seasoning – paprika, black pepper, a touch of salt and perhaps a sprinkle of chilli powder.

Method

1. Collect, pluck free of wings and legs, remove the intestines and wash your grasshoppers.

2. Coat them lightly with the olive oil or butter and lightly fry them with the seasoning.

3. Serve up while they are hot.

4. Enjoy! They go down nicely with a Mediterranean style salad and a glass of chilled white wine.

And Finally on Grasshoppers

Old Man: 'As quickly as you can, snatch the pebble from my hand. When you can take the pebble from my hand it will be time for you to leave.'

Several years and many hundred pebble snatch attempts later.

Old Man: 'Time for you to leave.'

Exit Grasshopper.

No explanation necessary – those that know, will know.

Ladybirds – Coccinellidae

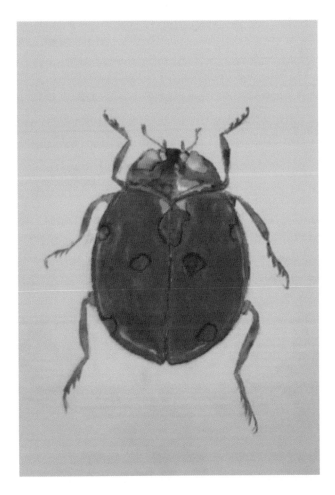

The Scarlet Lady

Worldwide, there are over 5000 species of Ladybirds. In Britain there are only 46 species. Of these, 26 are referred to as 'conspicuous' – that is, they sport bright markings, usually red and black polka dots, but other colours are available. The remaining species are known as 'inconspicuous' – this means that their colouring is drabber and more neutral, but whether colourful or neutral they are equally beautiful.

How Ladybirds arrived in Britain

In the Middle Ages there was a great travesty throughout the lands. Huge swarms of biting and chewing insects descended upon the islands and began to devour everything green in the fields. The crops were threatened - neither smoke nor sprays nor powders nor potions would eradicate the living plague. The people were staring into the face of starvation. There was nothing left to do but pray. Across the land prayers were said to Our Lady, The Virgin Mary, the mother of Jesus. Clouds gathered in the skies, and it began to rain, but this was a red rain, the like of which had never been seen before. It was a rain of insects with red shells and black spotted markings. The tiny red and black beetles attacked the crop-destroying insects and devoured them one by one, field by field. The crops were saved, the harvest was brought in, and national starvation was averted. The newcomer, life-saving insects were named by people as 'The Beetle of Our Lady', which in time became 'Lady Beetles,' and eventually 'Ladybirds'. They are still much loved across the nation and seen as a symbol of religious faith, loyalty and protection. In the recent past baby clothing was often marked with a tiny picture of a Ladybird.

Some Ladybird Folklore

If a Ladybird lands on your hands – news gloves are on the way. And you get to make a wish. In the direction it flies away you'll find your true love.

If a Ladybird lands on your head – a new hat! And as it flies away the pretty beetle will take with it any ailments you might have.

If you have toothache and cannot afford a dentist simply crush up some Ladybirds and stuff the mash into the cavity. Guaranteed as a cure in days of yore – but do remember that ill luck follows if you kill a Ladybird.

In the olden days colic and measles could be cured with a Ladybird potion, although dried, powdered and pipe-smoked Ladybirds are said to provoke nightmares.

On corn, if the number of spots is less than seven the harvest will be bountiful. If more than seven, crop failure and famine are most likely.

Silverfish – *Zygentoma*

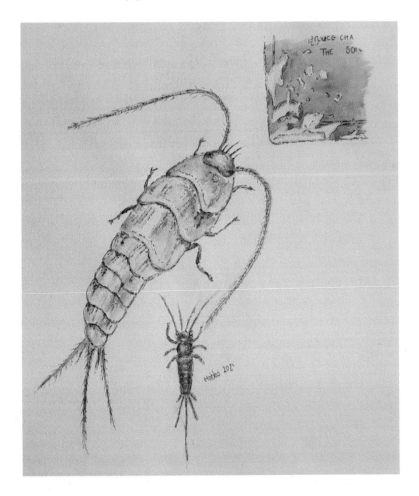

Also known as: bristletails, fishmoths, tarpums, jewfish.

The Silent Creature Unlike bees or butterflies, there are relatively few books written about or dedicated to silverfish. These creepy, quiet little critters keep themselves well hidden. They are usually spotted in the back forgotten corners of food cupboards or randomly emerge from the pages of a book. They barely define definition, and some experts declare, quite passionately, that they are not insects at all, for they are wingless. However, they are creepy, crawly, and harmless, so have earned their pages here. Also, they are believed to be the planets most ancient 'insects' and were flitting about here in the undergrowth millions of years before dinosaurs were dreamed up. They are declared a 'synanthropic' species by the aforementioned experts, a word that is worth their inclusion in this book alone. It means that they live in close association with human beings, whose cluttery, crummy homes provide them with an ideal habitat. They usually emerge at night to prowl about bathrooms, toilets and kitchens, feasting on organic debris and substances containing carbohydrates, sugars and starches that humans so carelessly and casually scatter around. They are often found between the pages of books and old newspapers, feasting away on the ink and pages. They seem to like old books and ancient manuscripts, especially in libraries and museums, where alas, their hungry bites do some serious damage to the pages. If subjected to sudden brightness (i.e., you switch the light on while going down to the kitchen for a glass of water in the middle of the night) they slither and swim away to the nearest dark corners. We here have not actually seen a silverfish in the flesh in years, so perhaps they are fading from existence. We hope not. But in years gone by, having seem them, and looked at them close up, despite their creepiness they are actually quite beautiful and elegant little things. Cybermats, however, are little more scary and dangerous versions of the creature, so watch out for those. They are small and deadly, able to move silently, leap onto their victims and bite them to death, and are impervious to hard objects or bullets. They can, however, be destroyed by the application of electricity or if exposed to gold. Cybermats, these deadly versions of silverfish, were first encountered on the planet Telos in The Tomb of the Cybermen. Let's hope a few of them don't slip out of the pages of this book and into your living room! We are talking Doctor Who talk here, of course, so do not be too alarmed. The deadly Cybermats in the Doctor Who series were inspired by the humble silverfish.

Silverfish – traditional medicine and culinary uses

There are few, if any, recorded reports of the use of silverfish in medicine or healing. No recipes for the use of them seem to be available although, like all insects, if collected in large amounts they would provide a harmless source of protein. Mashed, rolled into small balls with a touch of paprika, black pepper and garlic paste, they are potentially very tasty. They are said to taste like…. Well, a cross between fish and chicken, of course.

Traditional Tales about silverfish.
There are none! But we did find this fragment of a traditional rhyme from a poet based in Whitby, North Yorkshire:

Ode to Silverfish
In the back of the bottom food cupboard
Where nobody, nobody goes,
They hide and they lurk
And swim in the murk
Munching on old potatoes.
They lurk and they hide,
They slither and glide,
They come out at night to prowl 'round.
They're silver and fishy
And quite hard to squishy
So best just to leave on the ground.

Spiders – Arachnida

'Incy Wincy spider
Climbing up the spout,
Out came the rain drops
To wash the spider out,
Out came the sunshine
To drive away the rain,
Incy Wincy spider
Climbed the spout again.'
Bradford finger-play version of an international rhyme game.

As with butterflies, whole book could, should and will have been written about spiders. Technically speaking, arachnids are not insects, but they are quite creepy and crawly so will do for us here. What other tiny creature causes so much revulsion, dread, panic, or fear? And yet they are so tiny and beautiful. The next time you recoil or shriek or flee a room in panic at the sight of a spider remember this little trick to help you abate your dread or phobia. Take a normal or even large house spider. Set it down on the floor. Stand beside it. Imagine that you were the poor spider, and that some hideous incomprehensively vast and deadly creature was there beside you, towering into the sky. Now really, who should be afraid and recoiling in horror?

Spider folklore exists in every country and culture throughout the world. They are a symbol of mischief, malice, connectivity, fear, revulsion, and all things toxic. On the positive side, they are equated with patience and persistence due to their skill of setting elaborate and beautiful webs and then waiting for their prey.

Without spiders, your carpets, your bedding, your rugs, your baskets, your cushions and indeed your clothing would not exist – for of course, in most mythologies around the world, spiders are the source and inspiration of the craft of spinning weaving fabrics. Also, knot work and net making would not have existed without the inspiration of the spider's craft. Not to mention the World Wide Web!

Various deities, usually female, are linked to the spider. In ancient Egypt, the goddess Neith was known as the spinner and weaver of destinies. The same goddess by different names is known as Ishtar in ancient Babylonia, Arachne in Greece, and Minerva in Rome.

The Story of Athena and Arachne – the first spider

Although not technically a tale from British folklore, having evolved in Turkey (Lydia) and then come to our shores through the Greeks then the Romans, this is a moral tale well worth sharing. Perhaps, having read this, you will feel sorry for the next spider that you chance upon, wherever you are.

Arachne was a shepherd's daughter who began weaving at an early age. Her father was a wool dyer and fabric expert and through working for him she became a great weaver. People came from far and wide to look upon the amazing fabrics that she wove. All the praise and admiration went to her head. Foolishly, she began to boast that her skill as a weaver was even greater than the goddess Athena's. Athena, goddess of wisdom, handicraft and warfare, was always up for a contest. She took great offense at Arachne's boasting and, after disguising herself as an old woman, she set up a contest between the two of them. Presenting herself as the old lady, she approached the boasting girl and warned, 'My girl, you mortals can never compare to any of the gods. Plead for forgiveness and Athena might spare your soul.'

Arachne considered her latest work, a beautiful, shimmering piece that seemed like sunlight and water. 'Well, I only speak the truth,' she said. 'If Athena thinks otherwise then let her come down and challenge me.' Athena removed her disguise and appeared in her bright glory, clad in a white gown that sparkled like star light. Arachne was surprised, but not frightened. She set herself at her loom and the goddess set to at hers. The two began weaving straight away. Athena's weaving represented four separate contests between mortals and the gods in which the gods punished mortals for setting themselves as equals of the gods. Arachne's weaving depicted ways that the gods, particularly Zeus, had misled and abused mortals, tricking and seducing many mortal women. When

Athena saw that Arachne had not only insulted the gods but done so with a work far more beautiful than her own, she was enraged. She destroyed Arachne's tapestry and her loom, struck her about the head with the shuttle and cursed her to live with a sense of eternal guilt. Terrified and ashamed, Arachne hanged herself. However, Athena, showing some pity, or perhaps wanting to prolong her revenge, sprinkled a potion of poisons and herbs upon the hanging corpse. At the touch of this potion, Arachne's hair fell out. Her nose and ears and thumbs dropped off. Her head shrank and her whole body became quite tiny. Her fingers sprung out from her body as eight hairy legs. She became the first spider, and even to this day she and her descendants hide away in dark corners and spin threads from their bodies. As a spider, feared and reviled by most people, Arachne weaves her ancient and endless web to this very day.

Some Spider folklore

In Scotland, the story of Robert the Bruce and the persevering spider is much loved and well known. Back in the 1300's, Robert was fighting against the armies of the English king, trying to gain independence for Scotland. After several resounding military defeats – six to be precise - Robert had to retreat, then flee, then hide. While hiding away in a cave he noticed a spider trying to weave a web in a slippery corner of the entrance. Its first few attempts to secure its stands of the web failed utterly. It did not give up though, but went on trying until at last, on the seventh attempt, it wove a magnificent web that was soon capturing insects that would be the spider's food. Inspired by the creature's tenacity, Robert decided to come out of hiding and rally his troops to have another go at the English. The spider had taught him well. At the Battle of Bannockburn in 1314, against all odds, his army crushed the English. His forces at last defeated and drove away the invaders and Scottish independence was secured.

The ancient Celts and British pagans thought that spiders brought good luck. They would seek out and capture large spiders then keep them in a silk purse that was worn around the neck. This not only warded off illnesses but could attract wealth. Flies, small beetles and other bugs would be dropped into the purse to feed the 'lucky' spider. The webs of spiders were also used to stop bleeding. Collected up and jammed into the wound, they were guaranteed to stem the flow of blood.

It is still widely believed that humans swallow spiders in their sleep – up to four a year. This modern urban myth is apparently untrue. Spiders are very sensitive creatures, particularly to sound, so the noises and vibrations of a human sleeper, especially the breath from their mouths, would scare any spider away. During trials and experiments, scientists propped open the mouths of human volunteers and when they were sleeping covered their beds with a wide variety of spiders. Not one single spider was swallowed by the hundreds of volunteers over several nights of these tests. This just goes to show that, in the world of folklore, you cannot always believe what you hear or read.

Scorpions - Arachnida/scorpions

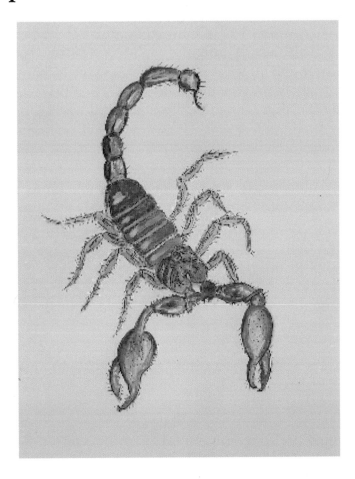

A close relative of the spider, also an arachnid, and not widely found in The British Isles, we thought we would include Scorpions here along with their eight-legged cousins. Widely thought of as desert or jungle dwelling creatures, Scorpions are actually found in the south of England, especially on the walls of ports, where they are believed to have been imported with boxes of fruit and tea. The best sites for finding them are the Isle of Sheppey in Kent and around the dockland town of Sheerness. Scorpions in general are associated with evil, human sexuality and painful deaths. Many varieties do have a nasty sting which can kill a human if there is an allergic reaction, but the British varieties are no more dangerous than a wasp. Scorpions are night feeders so you will rarely see them in daylight. They are also viviparous – that is to say, they give birth to their offspring, which is very rare for arachnids and insects.

As with spiders, scorpion venom is well known in folk medicine as a painkiller, in small doses of course. Along with most poisons, such as arsenic and opium, used in little amounts they are said to have beneficial properties for human health.

The Scorpion and The Frog – a fable from Kent

If you know anything about astrology, you will know that Scorpios, as well as being enigmatic, interested in all things dark and sexually irresistible, are also known for their cutting comments and barbed words. They know how to sting! They cannot help it; it is in their nature. They have many attributes of a scorpion, as this tale well illustrates: -

Once, on The Isle of Sheppey, a scorpion was on its way to visit its mother who had moved away from the dockland walls to the village of Minster further up the island. However, there had been a great deal of rain the few days previously.

Just before the village, where there had been a drainage ditch, there was now a river in full flow. Not to be thwarted and keen to see his mother, the scorpion looked for a way across the water. He saw a large frog basking on a stone on the riverbank.

'Hello sister,' he said. 'Do me a favour would you. Let me climb upon your back and then swim me across to the other side of this river. I'm on my way to visit my mother.'

The frog eyed the scorpion warily, for their reputation of treachery and venomous attacks had spread far and wide in the world of creatures.

'No way,' she croaked. 'You're a scorpion. You'll probably sting me to death and eat me for your supper.'

'I will not,' the scorpion assured her. 'I promise on my dear mother's life. And furthermore, for your troubles, I'll give you this...'

From a secret pouch within his chest the scorpion produced a beautiful diamond that glittered and shone in the sunlight. For as everybody knows, a scorpion always has a diamond secreted away about its person. Convinced by the scorpion's words and lured by the prize of a shining diamond, the frog agreed to carry him across the river. As they crossed, they chatted on like old friends, each telling the other about their lives. The frog rather wished that the scorpion were a frog, for he was funny and eloquent and there was something about him that she quite liked. Just before they reached the riverbank the scorpion raised his tail and stung the frog with its deadly venom.

'Ouch! Ouch! You promised not to sting me! Why did you do that?' cried the poor frog.

'Sorry,' said the scorpion taking back his diamond from the dying creature and putting it back into his pouch. 'I can't help it. It's in my nature.'

And with that he leapt onto the riverbank and hurried on his way to see his dear mother.

Sting alert!

The writer and the illustrator of this book are both Scorpios.

Slugs and Snails – Gastropoda

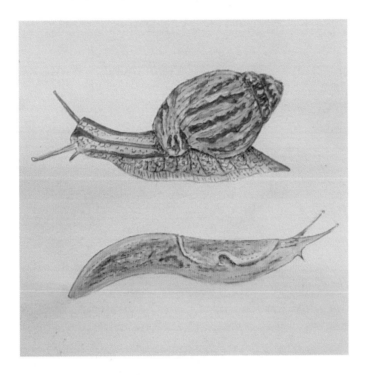

'What are little girls made of?
Sugar and spice and all things nice.
What are little boys made of?
Slugs and snails and puppy dogs' tails.'

Slug and Snail Folklore

Like many people, I have always had a cringing, shudder-inducing repulsion about slugs. But they are very beautiful when you put aside your prejudices and look closely. Snails I don't mind at all except when they devour my garden lettuce.

These creatures – gastropods, or 'stomach foots' - are said to bridge the world between the elemental worlds of Water and Earth, and in the olden days they were believed to be born directly out of clay. In some parts of the world, they are kept as pets and are said to make great and loving companions. Snail racing is a popular sport in the UK and there is a regular racing circuit where snails are raced on circular boards.

The shape of the snail shell replicates the patterns of the universe, the spirals of life, death and rebirth. The shell is also said to represent the rotation of our Earth around the sun. The Aztecs regarded them as sacred because one of their gods – Quetzalcoatl – wore a spiral shell upon his chest because he held the secrets to reincarnation and the mystical cycles of the universe. One of their other gods, Tecciztecatl – bore a snail upon his back to symbolize rebirth, which was linked to the phases of the disappearing and reappearing moon. In Christianity, however, slugs and snails were used as a symbol for one of the seven deadly sins – sloth. They were considered slow and lazy. As slow as a snail. Moving at a snail's pace. Snail mail etc.
The ancient Greek poet, Hesiod, was renowned for being able to predict the time to harvest wheat by watching the habits of slugs and snails. He believed that when they climbed, or slid, up the stems of the crop it was harvest time. Nerite, a minor deity, is the Greek god of snails.

Slugs were considered as beautiful, ethereal beings loaded with healing powers by Native Americans. Allegedly, they used them to cure toothache by popping live ones into their mouths and allowing them to wriggle around over the sore teeth and gums. As gruesome and unpleasant as this may sound, there is now a scientific basis for this cure. The slime of slugs and snails, collected by Native Americans and the ancient Greeks for its healing properties, has recently been discovered to have astringent and antiseptic properties. Slime is now regularly used medically in treatments for skin damage and burns. And, of course, beauty products for skin and facial products now abound with slime cures. Face packs sourced from slug and snail slime are apparently all the rage. Not believing? Check out the lists of skin care products on any health food shop worth its salt.

Slugs and Snails as Food

The Romans used to farm snails as a food product, and of course the French and Indonesians are well known for devouring them by the bucketload. In Bristol, in the poorer areas, they were once a vital source of protein and were known as 'wall fish'. They were regularly served as a snack in Bristol pubs and to children as a treat and even until the 1950's (and perhaps beyond) they were being collected in Clifton Park as a food source. 'Snailer Jack' of Victorian Bristol used to collect them widely and sell them as a food. Somehow the devouring of slugs and snails is always cloaked in pretty sounding language. Escargot. Often served as hors d'oeuvre (snail starter). Escargots a la Bourguignonnes (Snail stew with old bread). Sop Tutut (Indonesian snail soup). Heliciculture (snail farming). I have eaten snails – once. In Belfast, of course. They were nice – thanks to the creamy garlic sauce. Now, they are meant to be a very trendy dish, regularly featured by top TV chefs.

TOP TIP. If you are getting hungry reading this and you fancy some gastropods, you must prepare them first by cleaning, soaking and careful cooking. Eating them raw or underprepared can apparently be fatal, as William Foyle of Chippenham found out in 1937 after collecting dozens of snails from his greenhouse and eating them. Mrs. Foyle said in a newspaper article of the day that her husband had a 'hearty tea' of the snails which he had collected, cooked and cleaned himself. If only she had roasted him a pork chop! Well apparently, she had – for lunch. The coroner at his inquest suspected that this might have poisoned William, not the snails but this line of inquiry was never pursued, and Mrs. Foyle lived on to enjoy a long, happy widowhood.

Editors note: please see the publisher's disclaimer at the start of this book. The paragraph above is not a handy guide on how to discard of annoying, stupid or irritating husbands!

Wasps – Vespidae

The Wasp by Ogden Nash

The wasp and all his numerous family
I look upon as a major calamity.
He throws open his nest with prodigality,
But I distrust his waspitality.

A wasp is any insect of the narrow-waisted suborder Apocrita of the order Hymenoptera which is neither a bee nor an ant. They are perhaps the most reviled and hated of insects, certainly so in the British Isles. 'What is the point of wasps?' people bemoan. 'All they do is be annoying and sting people.'

But wasps, apart from being physically beautiful and a design masterpiece, are actually very useful creatures. They kill aphids and many other garden pests, and some species pollinate plants. Not being as hairy as their cousins, they are not as effective as pollinators as bees, but they are high up there on the list of plant assisting insects. Generally, wasps do not produce honey, apart from the Mexican Honey Wasps, which are not yet found in Britain. Wasps do like honey, however, along with most sweet or sugary food stuffs. They are quite happy to steal it from beehives as a food source.

Wasp stings are of course notoriously painful and linger on the skin for days and even weeks afterwards. I should know. Once, while pushing my son in his pushchair, one randomly flew down my shirt and stung me several times on the chest! The stings twinged and itched for many months afterwards. When a wasp stings it injects venom into your skin. Apparently, it is not the venom that causes pain and swelling. These are a result of your own body defenses kicking in to try and protect you against the venom, much the same as when feeling in ill when having a cold or flu like illnesses is a result of your immune system kicking in to combat the virus. So, the next time you get wasp-stung and are feeling the pain, blame yourself, not the nasty critters

Some Wasp Folklore - Bees, hornets, and wasps are all sacred to the ancient Egyptians. The Egyptian goddess, Ahti, had the body of a hippopotamus and the head of a wasp, and was known as Queen of the Wasps. She was not the most beautiful of goddesses and was believed to be vengeful, spiteful, a troublesome nuisance and a lover of chaotic disorder. Her sting could kill small children and they quite rightly lived in fear of her. Ahti was never represented on amulets, charms or artwork, and is now largely forgotten. A northern European tradition that seeped into American culture is The Christmas Wasp, which also has links to East Anglia and the Yorkshire Wolds. People used to bake cakes that were coloured black and yellow, known as *wasp cakes*, which were left out on the winter solstice, just before Christmas, to attract good luck and repel evil. In the Yorkshire Wolds, East Anglia and South Jutland, Denmark (closely related areas historically and racially), the ceremony of the JULEN HVEP is still maintained by some the families, with dark rye and light wheat cakes baked at Christmas to appease the ancient pagan Wasp King. The Wasp King (a giant angry wasp who inflicts random acts of cruelty) is interchangeable with the Christmas Wasp in European folklore stories, with one of his 'adventures' recorded in 'The Devil's Golden Fish' by the brothers Grim in their 1812 collection of folk and fairy tales. We won't repeat the tale here, but here's a quick paraphrase: - A farmer prays that his son can escape poverty by becoming a lawyer. The devil hears his prayer and tells him that he can make the prayer come true in exchange for his soul. They end having a dispute over a turnip crop that ends with the devil claiming the farmer's soul anyhow. The farmer makes several offers to hold onto his soul, including cutting off his own fingers with red-hot iron scissors in. The devil refuses his offers and is only interested when the farmer says he can lead him to the best honey ever tasted. The devil, who has a bit of a sweet tooth, is interested and accepts the offer. That Yuletide, the farmer leads the Devil to a wasps' nest in his barn and invites the devil to put in his hand and collect the delicious honey. Stupidly, the devil does so, for as everybody now knows, wasps do not produce honey. A giant wasp, The Wasp King, angrily appears from the nest and proceeds to sting the devil all over, driving him back to Hell. The farmer then attempts to persuade the obviously magical wasp if he could conjure him up a donkey that would spill silver coins from its moth every time that it brayed. The Wasp King, somewhat irritated by the annoying and foolish farmer, stung the farmer to death and went to live in a crack in an elm tree. The son, who started all the trouble anyway, moves away to Hamburg where he leads a life of poverty as an unsuccessful tailor. Oh – those Brothers Grim. No happy ending there then.

Late nineteenth and early twentieth century depictions of the Wasp King with a Santa hat on are of American origin, and these were largely to promote a brand of cola - McCarthy's Cola, of Pennsylvania, around 1920 – 'The cola with a sting in its tail'. The Christmas Wasp and the Wasp King are now largely forgotten, along with McCarthy's Cola – the company went bankrupt in 1921 soon after their Christmas Wasp advertising campaign.

Some Top Wasp Tips

The best way to treat a wasp sting is to dab it with baking powder or apply a paste of the same and avoid rubbing or scratching the affected area.

Unless you are 'handy' do not try to remove wasps' nest yourself. If unsuccessful you will be attacked by a swarm of wasps and chased by them as far as you can run! Get an expert in.

To have a wasp-free picnic place a very ripe, opened banana just away from your picnic area. Wasps love a ripe banana and will be much more interested in that than you and your food.

If stung by a wasp:
Wash the affected area with soap and water. Apply an ice pack to the skin. Apply an antihistamine cream onto the sting for a quick relief. Do not scratch the area no matter how itchy it is. This way, you will prevent swelling and will reduce the pain

DO NOT apply vinegar or lemon juice, despite the folklore. These can make the sting even more painful. Applications of garlic, onions, tea tree oil and human spittle are also largely ineffective.

In Cornwall, following the 'jellyfish sting principle', people stung by a wasp often call out to the nearest person, friend or stranger, requesting for them to urinate over the afflicted area, firmly believing that human urine will relieve the pain. This, however, is not a recommended cure on grounds of social etiquette and the actual pain-relieving ineffectiveness of urine. So, if in Cornwall and you hear the cry of, 'Hey, you there, piss on my sting!', we advise that you ignore the plea and just keep walking.

Woodlice – Isopoda

Also known as Coffin Cutters, Parson's Pigs, Roly Polys, Cheesy Bobs. Sow Bugs, Pill Bugs, Billy Baker, Monkey Pea, Grammer Sows, Chiggy Wig, Cheese Log, Granny Grunters, Dampers, Hardy Backs, Penny Sow... well, the list could fill the page.

There are over 250 localized nicknames for these charming and harmless little critters, many linked to pigs, which somehow, they were once thought to resemble.

Technically, woodlice are not insects at all, but crustaceans, related to crabs, shrimps, prawns and lobsters. They are the only known land-based crustacean and breathe through something resembling gills. They are even said to taste like prawns when cooked – but more of that later. Little, harmless, unassuming and edible – what more could you want from a bug? They are even said to make good pets for people who do not have time for cats and dogs. They can be kept in an old fish tank or transparent plastic container with a layer of compost or leaf litter, and they will happily live off kitchen peelings or vegetable food waste. They can be left unsupervised for weeks on end – ideal if you want to leave your pets at home while you go on holiday.

Unlikely as it seems, woodlice racing was until quite recently a popular sport. The legendary 'William', thought to be a sure winner, was allegedly drugged and tampered with in a key race in 1978 – at the time of writing the race and commentary is still there on YouTube. Ideally, the racing woodlice are lightly marked with paint to identify their owner, placed into a glass and upturned onto a board marked with concentric circles. The first runner to cross the outer circle is the winner. Richard Child Willis, the 19th century owner of Ravenshill Hall just outside Whitby, North Yorkshire, squandered his vast inherited fortune on horse and woodlice racing. Rudyard Kipling, whose family lived nearby, was also a great fan of the sport.

Woodlice – medicinal and culinary uses

In 1885, Vincent Holt, a social engineer, advocated the eating of 'woodland produce' by the poor to alleviate food shortages and hunger. He meant insects, of course. He advised an 'excellent fish sauce', which consisted of woodlice, lightly boiled, added to butter, flour, salt and pepper. He claimed that it was quite delicious. When lightly fried, true to their crustacean origins, they are said to taste just like shrimps.

In Gloucestershire they were eaten as a cure against rickets. Three hundred live woodlice were stirred into twelve pints of light ale together with raisins, rhubarb and fern roots. The delicious potion was eagerly imbibed, and the drinkers felt instantly better.

Living woodlice in a bag tied around a baby's neck were said to alleviate teething pains and cure smallpox. Swallowed live, they could also cure whooping cough and constipation. Members of the gentry with 'costive bowels' dried and pulverized them then dissolved the powder in Rhenish wine. Imbibed with gusto, it was said to vastly improve the flavour of the German wine while also curing bowel blockages, jaundice, ague and failing eyesight.

Some biological curiosities

Woodlice have an unusual lung system, linked to their crustacean ancestry. Some have 7 pairs of lungs, some have 2 pairs and some none at all, but a sort of half formed set of under-gills. The females have 2 vaginas, both of which must be 'serviced' to ensure pregnancy. The new-born centipedes are carried in inner pouches in which the young develop before emerging as the tiny woodlice that can be seen under garden logs and stones. They always have fourteen legs, seven on either side. It is said to be a sign of ill-luck if you find a thirteen-legged woodlouse, hence most people are disinclined to upturn them and do a leg count.

Worms – Annelida

'The smallest worm will turn, being trodden on....'
Henry 6th Part 3, William Shakespeare

Last but not least – the humble worm. Human beings, and this planet as we know it, would not exist without them.

With over 22 000 living worm species, including Australian giant Gippsland earthworms and giant African Jungle Worms (over 3 ft long but able to extend up to ten feet and as thick as a child's wrist) and parasitic microscopic species, worms deserve a book in their own right. As it is, we will just have to skim the slimy surface of them here. In Britain, earthworms and the red wiggle are the most common types. There are some colourful localized names for the little wrigglers: manure worm, redworm, branding worm, night crawlers, angleworm (fishing bait), dew-worm, rain wriggles, panfish, trout worm, tiger worm, red wiggler. The slow worm, though beautiful, sleek and elegant, is in fact a reptile, a legless lizard, so that is the only look-in it will get here. Worms are divided into ringed segments. They have five hearts. They have no eyes and sense light, or 'visualise', through their skin. Their skin exudes a lubricating fluid which makes their passage through subterranean burrows and across soil easier. Prolonged exposure to light leads to their paralysis and the drying out of this essential lubricant – in effect, light kills them. They are one of the most important creatures on the planet, breaking down animal dung, dead and rotting animal matter and decaying vegetation, as they feed. Basically, they are a digestive tube enclosed within a segmented tube, eating and disposing of up a third of their body weight each day, redistributing essential minerals and nutrients that are essential to healthy, plant growing soil. Quite simply, the plant-bearing planet as we know it could not function or survive without worms.

Annelida is from the Latin word anellus, meaning 'little ring', the majority of the species being ringed or segmented in physical structure. Worms often trigger off an instinctive shuddering response of repulsion in many people. They are not the nation's favourite creepy-crawly, possibly because some people are repelled by the idea that they happily devour us once we are done and dusted and buried in the ground. As the tragically dying (and somewhat wordy) Mercutio declares to Benvolio in Shakespeare's 'Romeo and Juliet': 'They have made worms' meat of me!'

Some Worm Folklore

In folklore, there is some confusion to the word 'wyrms' and 'worms'. There are many old British tales of 'wyrms' – the word (Old English/Saxon root) originally meant anything with a long body and no legs, and became inter-connected with serpents and mythological limbless, but sometimes winged, dragons. Here we will set these 'wyrms' aside as a separate strand of folklore – but anybody with an interest might look up the fabulous tales of Nordic and Saxon 'wyrms', which include of course the wonderful tale of 'The Lampton Worm'. One read of that, and you might never go fishing on a Sunday again. Other British 'wyrm' yarns include The Worm of Sockborn, The Worm of Linton and The Laidly Worm of Bamburgh. As a folkloric point of interest, it is believed that these Nordic/Saxon related 'wyrm' tales, like the nationwide black dog stories, relate to bands of marauding Viking, the 'wyrm', or 'dragon', being in fact a symbolic metaphor for a band of destructive invaders that has become embedded in a local tale of death, pillaging and destruction.

If only Mongolia was in the British Isles! Then we could regale you with tales of The Mongolian Death Worm, a huge intestinal, sausage-like worm, up to 5 feet long and bright blood red that creeps into its hosts body, sets itself up in the stomach and grows – and grows. The stomach expands and distends, and no purges or laxatives can un-hinge it. Eventually the swollen belly explodes, killing the host. The liberated, nourished, acid-spitting Death Worm winds its way to safety and seclusion in the dunes of The Gobi Desert, ready to spawn its young, who will patiently await to infest their next human victims. Several well-known films and works of fiction have borrowed heavily of this true-life scenario.

It is true that if you cut through a worm, it can regrow its tail – but only if you chop it below its clitella, the distinct fleshy ring on its body, above which all of its 5 hearts exist. Slice between the clitella and the head and there will be no miraculous re growth – just a poor little dead creature.

Worm Sex

Worms are gender-fluid hermaphrodites, simultaneously existing as male and female, producing both eggs and sperm, though not able to reproduce with themselves. They mate on the exposed ground, pressing their bodies together to exchanges eggs and sperm before separating and wending on their ways. A fleshy ring is formed, (the clitella), filled with eggs and sperm, and this drops off, becoming a cocoon for the developing fertilized eggs. The baby worms later emerge tiny but fully formed and ready to eat. The average lifespan of a worm is two years, although in worm farms they have been known to live for up to eight years.

Worms as Food

Of course, worms have long been recognised as a potential food source, even if they are not yet in everybody's culinary repertoire. They are high in protein, have high levels of iron and amino acids, with properties that help break down foods and repair damaged body tissue. Earthworms also contain copper, manganese, zinc and calcium – all essential elements in a human diet, and especially beneficial for children and teenagers. Prepared correctly, worms are healthier than cheese, cow's milk, eggs and beef burgers. Many cultures around the world regularly add dried or fresh worms to tasty dishes, and the Mopane worm of Zambia and Zimbabwe is said to be particularly delicious (although, strictly speaking the Mopane is the tree dwelling caterpillar of the Emperor Moth so not really a worm at all). For those of you who are busy or in a hurry who want a quick fix worm dish to give your children or loved ones tonight, here is a sure hit dish – just collect your spade and get down to the park or garden for fifteen minutes or so of hard digging: -

Great British Worm Burgers

2 lb (900 grams) of freshly chopped worms (preferably common earthworm and red wiggle blend). Ideally, soak freshly caught worms overnight and drain before cooking to remove toxins.

Add 1 large pinch of paprika, cumin and mixed dried British herbs.

Splash in 2-3 dashes of Worcestershire sauce.

Spray down 2 Tbsp. of chopped or hand ripped coriander (fresh Bristol grown if available).

Whack in 2 whisked egg yolks – preferably from free-range Scottish eggs.

Slash through with I - 3 Tbsp of Suffolk rapeseed oil (although foreign sourced olive oil will suffice).

Add a small chuck of salt, black pepper and Bradford chili powder to taste.

Place all ingredients in a bowl and rough mix with bare hands. Shape the mixture with hands or metal burger rings. Lightly fry in a large frying pan for 6- 8 minutes on each side or until browned and sizzling. Before serving ensure that the burgers are piping hot throughout. Serve in a toasted bun with tomatoes, green salad leaf, chutney garnish and skinny chips. If BBQing, flip regularly to avoid burning.

Enjoy!

**Other books by Chris Firth
from Electraglade Press:**

Ghost Stories From Whitby – The Mulgrave Tales

Hocus Focus Hullabaloo (urban myths and legends)

Strange Whitby Tales – Whitby spooks and ghosts

The Fairies and Merfolk of North Yorkshire
(also illustrated by Rebecca Hobbs)

All available on-line or best ordered in bookshops.

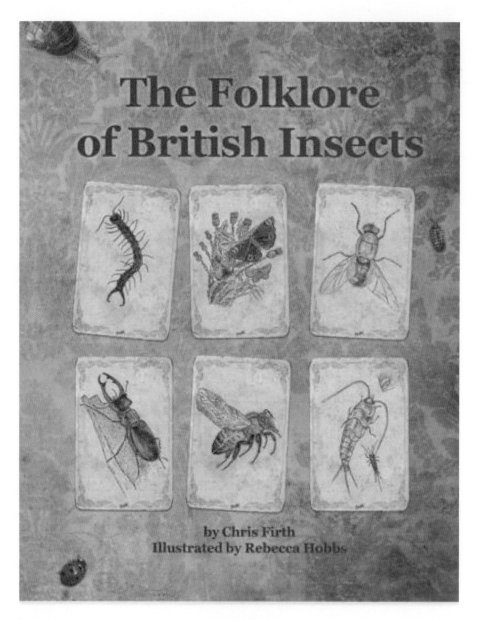

The Folklore
of British Insects

by Chris Firth
Illustrated by Rebecca Hobbs

Original cover image from first edition –
Graham Ambler (design) and Rebecca Hobbs (illustrator)

Printed in Great Britain
by Amazon